CESAR
CHAVEZ
CRUSADER FOR SOCIAL CHANGE

SPECIAL LIVES IN HISTORY THAT BECOME

Signature LIVES

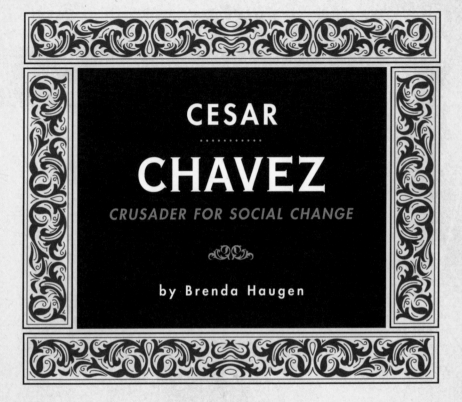

CESAR
CHAVEZ
CRUSADER FOR SOCIAL CHANGE

by Brenda Haugen

Content Adviser: Louis M. Holscher, J.D., Ph.D.,
Professor and Chair, Mexican American Studies,
San Jose State University

Reading Adviser: Rosemary G. Palmer, Ph.D.,
Department of Literacy, College of Education,
Boise State University

Compass Point Books ✦ Minneapolis, Minnesota

Compass Point Books
3109 West 50th Street, #115
Minneapolis, MN 55410

Visit Compass Point Books on the Internet at *www.compasspointbooks.com*
or e-mail your request to *custserv@compasspointbooks.com*

Editor: Julie Gassman
Page Production: Bobbie Nuytten
Photo Researcher: Svetlana Zurkin
Cartographer: XNR Productions, Inc.
Library Consultant: Kathleen Baxter

Art Director: Jaime Martens
Creative Director: Keith Griffin
Editorial Director: Nick Healy
Managing Editor: Catherine Neitge

Library of Congress Cataloging-in-Publication Data
Haugen, Brenda.
  Cesar Chavez: crusader for social change / by Brenda Haugen.
    p. cm.
  Includes bibliographical references and index.
  ISBN-13: 978-0-7565-3321-2 (library binding)
  ISBN-10: 0-7565-3321-X (library binding)
1. Chavez, Cesar, 1927—Juvenile literature. 2. Labor leaders—United
States—Biography—Juvenile literature. 3. Mexican American migrant
agricultural laborers—Biography—Juvenile literature. 4. United Farm
Workers—History—Juvenile literature. I. Title.
  HD6509.C48H38 2007
  331.88'13092—dc22 [B]   2007003939

MODERN AMERICA

Life in the United States since the late 19th century has undergone incredible changes. Advancements in technology and in society itself have transformed the lives of Americans. As they adjusted to this modern era, people cast aside old ways and embraced new ideas. The once silenced members of society—women, minorities, and young people—made their voices heard. Modern Americans survived wars, economic depression, protests, and scandals to emerge strong and ready to face whatever the future holds.

Table of Contents

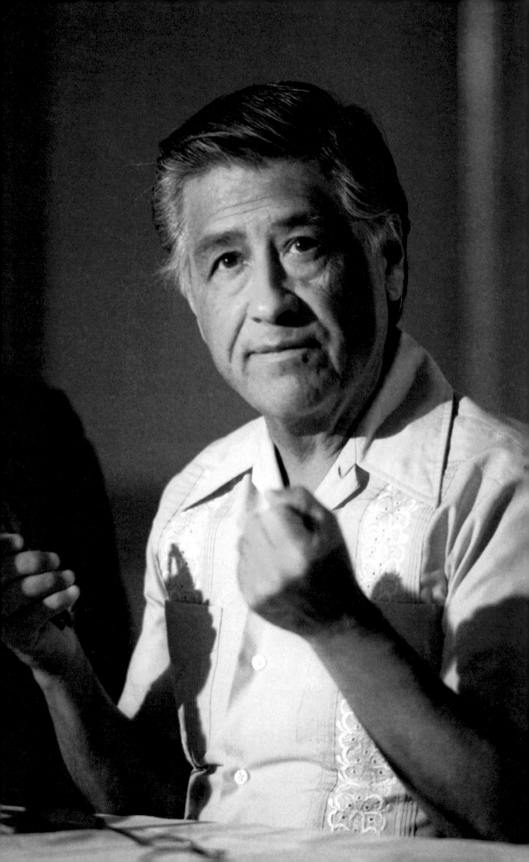

1 FINDING HIS PURPOSE IN LIFE

෴

Cesar Chavez was tired of social workers and community organizers coming around and asking silly questions. They said they wanted to improve conditions in underprivileged areas of the city. Though their hearts may have been in the right place, they never seemed to do any good for him and the others in his neighborhood. Chavez lived in a southeast San Jose, California, barrio, a Spanish speaking poor area of town. It was called *Sal Si Puedes*—Spanish for "get out if you can." The social workers asked their questions and then just went away. The people who lived in the barrio were no better off because they had answered the questions. They were just forgotten again.

When a man named Fred Ross of the Community

During his 30 years as a union leader, Cesar Chavez worked tirelessly to improve conditions for U.S. farmworkers.

Service Organization came looking for him in June 1952, Chavez figured he was just another do-gooder who would not do any good at all. Chavez was not interested. He told his wife, Helen, to tell Ross he was not home. Meanwhile, he would hide across the street at his brother Richard's home.

Helen did not like being dishonest, but she honored her husband's wishes. However, Ross was persistent. When he discovered Chavez was not home, he said he would return the next night. Again Chavez was gone, and again Ross promised to return the next evening. Helen grew tired of covering for her husband. Ross seemed like a nice man. She thought he might be able to help the people of Sal Si Puedes.

Chavez still had his doubts but knew he could not ask his wife to keep covering for him. Instead, he came up with another plan. He would invite some of the tough guys from the neighborhood to his meeting with Ross. Chavez developed a signal. When he moved a cigarette from one hand to the other, one of the tough guys would stand up and demand that Ross leave quickly and not return.

From the time he arrived that evening, Ross was made to feel unwelcome. Chavez greeted him with a limp handshake.

"When I put my hand toward Cesar, instead of getting up, he just sort of rocked forward on his behind, raising it an inch or two off the couch," Ross said. "When he shook my hand, it felt like a small piece of pig's liver."

But once Ross began to speak, Chavez realized Helen was right. Ross was different from the others. He knew about the problems of the people living in Sal Si Puedes. He realized children in the neighborhood had sores on their legs and feet from a creek that was polluted by waste from a fruit-packing shed. He knew that Mexican-Americans sometimes suffered beatings by the police. He knew about unsafe conditions that Mexican-Americans lived in every day. Perhaps even more important, he offered a way to help—the Community Service Organization.

In the 1950s, the CSO was active in 22 communities. Fred Ross (center, front row), Cesar Chavez (front row, second from right), and Cesar's wife, Helen, (back row, third from right) were important members.

The Community Service Organization was started in 1947 in East Los Angeles, California. The group was formed because of frustration about the way Mexican-Americans were treated. Mexican-American activists also wanted a say in government. Among their frustrations was the defeat of Edward Roybal. Though he was qualified and popular, Roybal was defeated in his bid for a Los Angeles City Council seat in 1947. This led activists to form the CSO and to conduct voter-registration drives in an effort to get Mexican-American candidates elected to office.

Members of the CSO were registering Mexican-American voters. The hope was that these new voters would elect candidates who would help Mexican-Americans. Ross was looking for someone in Sal Si Puedes to help register voters.

Chavez listened closely. He forgot all about the cigarette signal.

"Fred did such a good job of explaining how poor people could build power that I could taste it. I could really feel it," Chavez later said. "I thought, Gee, it's like digging a hole; there is nothing complicated about it."

Ross could tell he had ignited something in Chavez's soul. He immediately invited Chavez to another meeting that evening in East San Jose.

That night, Ross wrote in his diary: "I think I've found the guy I'm looking for."

Ross was right. Chavez was hooked. The 25-year-old who had been hiding now volunteered to knock on doors and ask people to register to vote.

Cesar Chavez organized and inspired farmworkers to use peaceful means to gain fair treatment and rights. Today a statue of Chavez honors his legacy in California State University, Fresno's Peace Garden.

Voter registration became the first step in Chavez's lifelong battle to improve the lives of Mexican-Americans, particularly migrant farm-workers. Chavez's name and work would gain attention, first in California and then across the nation. He would prove that a man, regardless of his background, could make a difference. ✒

13 ◌◌

2 EARLY LIFE LESSONS

❧❀❧

Cesar Estrada Chavez was born March 31, 1927, in the North Gila Valley of Arizona, near the borders of Mexico and California.

Cesar was the second of five children born to Librado and Juana Chavez. After living in an apartment for a time, the family moved to Librado's childhood home, an adobe farmhouse built by Librado's father, Cesario, near Yuma, Arizona.

Librado was one of 15 children in his family. As Librado's siblings grew up, they moved on to find their own ways in the world. Librado was the only one who continued to work on their father's 80-acre (32-hectare) farm.

In 1924, Librado married Juana Estrada. Along with farming, the couple ran a grocery store with an

During the Great Depression of the 1930s, thousands of migrant farmworkers headed to California in search of employment.

15 ❧

attached pool hall and a garage where gasoline was sold. They lived in an apartment above the store. The Chavezes worked hard, but they were happy.

In 1925, the Chavezes welcomed their first child, Rita, to the world. Two years later, Cesar was born. As their family grew, Librado and Juana passed on their beliefs and values to their children. Librado was strict and expected to be obeyed. However, he had a tender side and showed his children he loved them. He also taught his sons, Cesar and his younger brother Richard, how to run the farm. He showed them how to irrigate the dry Arizona land to grow crops such as watermelon, squash, and corn.

Juana also enjoyed spending time with her children. She played games with them and taught them about their Catholic faith. She also taught her children *dichos*—Mexican sayings—such as, "What you do to others, others do to you." These were more than just words to Juana. She often sent her children to look for the poor and homeless, and she opened her kitchen to them. No one would ever

The hot, dry climate around Yuma, Arizona, once kept the area from having the rich farmland it has today. Average high temperatures from early June through mid-September—the prime growing season—are above 100 degrees Fahrenheit (38 degrees Celsius). In the early 1900s, irrigation systems were built in the area, allowing farmers to water the dry soil, which received little rainfall. Today the area prospers from produce such as citrus fruit, lettuce, and wheat.

go hungry if Juana had something to share.

On the farm, Cesar and his siblings had space to run and play. Their favorite spot was a tree where they built forts, bridges, barns, and anything else they could imagine.

Cesar and Richard also helped at the family's store and garage. They waited on customers and pumped gas. In their spare time, the brothers could be found at the family's pool hall. Many nights were filled with the sharp, loud sounds of pool balls striking one another as the boys played game after game.

After the stock market crashed in 1929, Americans flocked to banks to pull out their money. Often it was too late.

Their carefree lives came to an end when the stock market crashed in October 1929. Thousands

of stock owners lost huge amounts of money when the value of their stocks nosedived. A worldwide economic slump called the Great Depression followed in the 1930s. Banks, factories, and other businesses closed. Millions of people lost their jobs and their homes.

In earlier years, the Chavez family had allowed customers to buy items from their store on credit. Customers took the goods and promised to pay for them later. During the Great Depression, however, many people could not pay their bills at the store. The Chavez family fell into debt, and by 1932, they were forced to sell their grocery store, pool hall, and garage.

But they still had their farm. Though the farmhouse lacked electricity and running water, the house was filled with love. The Chavezes raised chickens and grew vegetables. They would not go hungry.

Then in 1933, drought dried up the irrigation canals that brought water from the Colorado River to the Chavezes' fields. Without a crop to sell, the family could not pay its taxes. They owed $3,600. In the coming years, the debt would grow. Librado decided he had to find a way to make money or risk losing his family's farm. In 1938, he traveled to California. Librado had heard about jobs in Oxnard, a town north of Los Angeles, and he hoped to earn enough to pay his debt.

Work in the fields around Oxnard was plentiful, and many poor people were willing to do it. Because so many people desperately needed jobs, work in the fields did not pay well. Anyone complaining about the wages could easily be replaced.

Once he secured work, Librado asked his family to leave their farm for a time and join him in California. Juana and two adult relatives packed up her belongings and prepared her five children for the journey. Having never traveled far from home,

Oxnard was about 285 miles (456 kilometers) from the Chavez family farm near Yuma.

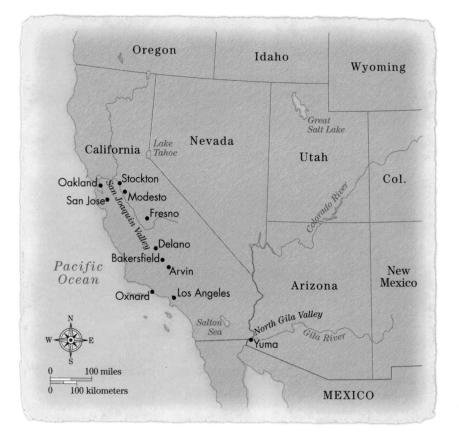

11-year-old Cesar was excited about this new adventure.

Cesar and his siblings drifted off to sleep as the adults drove through the night. Without warning, the sleeping children were jolted awake by very bright lights. The family feared the worst—being forced to leave the United States and go to Mexico.

"Suddenly two cars bore down on us, " Cesar remembered later.

> Uniformed men piled out of the cars and surrounded ours. We were half-asleep, all scared, and crying. It was the border patrol, our first experience with any kind of law. Roughly they asked for identification, our birth certificates, proof of American citizenship. ... My mother must have died a hundred times that night.

The frightened Chavezes were questioned for hours before they were finally allowed to drive on to Oxnard. Once there, the family continued to struggle. They lived in a rundown old shack and barely had enough food to survive. They often searched for wild mustard greens to avoid starvation.

A skilled crafter, Juana sold crocheted items in the street to earn money for gas, so the family could follow the cotton harvest. Like other migrant farmworkers, the Chavezes went from field to field. When the harvest was done on one farm, they traveled to

Migrant workers often had no more than tents for shelter.

the next, hoping to find work. But unlike most of the other farmworkers, the Chavezes still had a permanent home to return to in Arizona.

As an adult, Cesar remembered his family's home in Arizona:

> *I bitterly missed the ranch. I couldn't get used to the fences; we couldn't play like we used to. On the farm we had little places where we played, and a tree and we played there. We built bridges and we left everything there and when we came back the next day it was still there. You see, we never knew what stealing was, or to be stolen from. Then we went to the city and we left a ball outside for just a second and boom!—it was gone.*

Despite their hard work, the Chavezes made little money that summer. When they returned home to Arizona, they were no better off than when they had left. Still hoping to save his father's farm, Librado asked the governor for help. He found no assistance and could not pay the required taxes. When Cesar was 11, the deputy sheriff evicted the Chavez family, ordering them to leave their farm.

"We were pushed off the land," Cesar said. "When we left the farm, our whole life was upset, turned upside down. We had been part of a very stable community, and we were about to become migratory

workers. We had been uprooted."

At first, Librado, Juana, and the children often talked about earning enough money to reclaim the farm. Through the years they held onto that dream but quit talking about it. Sadly, that dream would never come true. ᕲᕳ

Chavez's beloved childhood home had been built out of adobe bricks in 1909. In the 1960s, just a few outside walls remained.

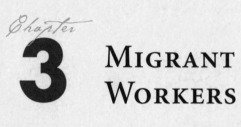

3 MIGRANT WORKERS

❧❧❧

After they lost their home, the Chavezes returned to California to work in the fields. They had no options other than to become permanent migrant farmworkers. They cared for and harvested a variety of crops, from strawberries, sugar beets, and tomatoes to lettuce, grapes, and cotton.

All field work was difficult, but some crops posed more hardships than others. Cesar hated harvesting broccoli. This harvest took place in the winter, when the ground was wet and slippery. Cesar would always remember how his shoes sank into the California mud. His hands ached with cold as he cut through the broccoli's tough stalks.

Jobs that required the use of a short-handled hoe were among the most difficult. Called *el cortito* ("the

The children of migrant farmworkers often went without schooling and joined their parents in the fields.

short one"), this type of hoe was used to thin lettuce and sugar beets—removing some of the plants to create more space for the remaining plants to grow. Growers required the short-handled hoe because they believed workers could not be as exact with the long-handled hoe. Because of the short handle, the migrants had to stay bent at the waist as they worked. This position quickly became very painful.

Working with the short-handled hoe could lead to lifelong back pains.

"You have to walk twisted, as you're stooped over, facing the row, and walking perpendicularly to it," Cesar said later. "You are always trying to find the best position because you can't walk completely sideways, it's too difficult."

Growers who used migrant farmworkers rarely tried to make their jobs easier. Few provided clean drinking water, time to rest, or toilets. Those who provided shelter for their workers rarely offered anything more than dirty shacks with no running water or electricity. Farmworkers who had tents considered themselves lucky.

The only thing more difficult than the work was arriving at a field and finding that the harvest was finished. Cesar and his family often went to bed hungry as they searched for work. But Librado taught his children that no job was worth losing their self-respect. If they, or other workers, were treated disrespectfully, they left the job—no matter how much they needed the money. Cesar recalled:

> *If any family felt something was wrong and stopped working, we immediately joined them, even if we didn't know them. And if the grower didn't correct what was wrong, then they would leave, and we'd leave. We weren't afraid to strike.*

Although Cesar had attended school in Arizona, he had little time for it anymore. He only went when his family did not need his help working in the fields. Because migrant farmworkers earned so little, the family needed everyone to contribute just to survive.

Mexican-American students were constantly reminded to speak English while at school.

In California, Cesar attended at least 36 schools as his family moved from one crop to the next. Some schools were segregated. White students went to one school, while black and Mexican-American students went to another.

Whether the schools were segregated or not, Cesar felt like a second-class citizen in most of them. Teachers seemed to doubt his intelligence because he was a Mexican-American. Some punished or humiliated Mexican-American students for speaking Spanish rather than English. They were not allowed to speak Spanish even while they played on the school grounds at recess. Other students sometimes made fun of migrant workers' children because they were poor and could not afford fancy clothes or nice shoes. Cesar's sister Rita loved school but dropped out when she was 12. The Chavezes could not afford to buy her shoes, and she was too embarrassed to go to school with bare feet.

"In integrated schools, where we were the only Mexicans, we were like monkeys in a cage," Cesar said. "There were lots of racist remarks that still hurt my ears when I think of them. And we couldn't do anything except sit there and take it."

In 1942, after finishing the eighth grade, Cesar also quit school. Despite his mother's protests, Cesar decided to work full time. His father had been hurt in a car accident, and Cesar felt he needed to work now more than ever. Later on, he regretted his lack of education, but at the time he believed he was doing what was necessary for his family.

As the family moved around California looking for work, they often found themselves in the small town of Delano. Here, in the middle of the San Joaquin Valley, they often found work. In 1943, Cesar also found his future wife in Delano.

Helen Fabela was 15 when she first met Cesar at a malt shop in Delano. Her father had died, and, like Cesar, she was working in the fields to help her

The San Joaquin Valley, in south-central California, has some of the world's richest land. It ranks as the state's top-producing agricultural region. Because of the crops that are grown there, the area is often called the "nation's salad bowl." Long, sunny summer days make it the perfect place to grow grapes, lettuce, peas, peaches, peppers, pears, and other crops. Today more than 2 million people live in the region, which includes cities such as Fresno, Modesto, Bakersfield, and Stockton.

family. Though the Chavezes moved to Sacramento to harvest tomatoes that summer, Cesar found Helen again when they returned in the fall. She also worked at the malt shop and at the People's Market. In his spare time, Cesar could be found at the market, too. He had fallen in love.

Cesar did not want to work in the fields all his life. He wanted something more. In 1944, near the end of World War II, he joined the Navy. Cesar hoped to learn skills he could use after the war. However, he quickly found he would not learn anything that would help him in civilian life, and he had no hope of advancing in the Navy. Mexican-Americans were only allowed to work as deckhands or painters.

Cesar later described his two years in the Navy as the worst years of his life. Serving on a ship, he was seasick most of the time. Eventually he was transferred to Guam, where he worked as a painter.

After being discharged from the Navy in 1946, Cesar returned to California. He took work

In 1942, Cesar earned an eighth grade diploma at age 15. Two years later he joined the Navy.

wherever he could find it. He tended and harvested grapes and cotton. For a while, he worked in the forests of northern California.

The newlyweds spent their honeymoon traveling the California coast.

On October 22, 1948, he married his sweetheart, Helen Fabela, in a church in San Jose. Driving a borrowed car, the newlyweds enjoyed a two-week honeymoon, visiting several Catholic missions in California. After their trip, the Chavezes returned to Delano. They soon started a family. A son, Fernando, was born in 1949, and a daughter, Sylvia, followed a year later. By 1959, they had welcomed six more children—Linda, Eloise, Anna, Elizabeth, Paul, and Anthony—into their poor but loving home.

In the early 1950s, the Chavezes settled in San Jose in the poor area known as Sal Si Puedes. Most of the people living in this barrio worked in nearby fields and orchards.

Cesar was disappointed that his military service had not helped him improve his situation. He slaved in the fields, just as he had done before the war. However, something unexpected was about to happen. He would soon meet two people who would change his life forever. ❧

4 FIGHTING FOR SOCIAL JUSTICE

Thanks to his mother, Cesar Chavez found strength in his Catholic faith. It also led him to a man who would become his close friend.

A priest named Father Donald McDonnell met Chavez while visiting Sal Si Puedes in 1952. The energetic young priest reached out to Catholics in the area. He wanted to know whether they would support a church there. Chavez's family had to travel across town to a Portuguese church to attend Mass, the Catholic church service. Chavez was excited by the idea of having a church in his neighborhood. He volunteered to help McDonnell fix up an old neighborhood hall where church services could be held.

McDonnell felt strongly that all people should be treated with respect, regardless of their skin color,

During the 1950s, the Catholic Church reached out to farmworkers. One way to do this was to celebrate Mass in the fields.

Braceros were eager to arrive in the United States. They were transported on government-supplied trains.

background, education, or other traits. He wanted the Catholic Church to reach out to the poor and abandoned, including the Mexican braceros of California.

The braceros were laborers who came to California from Mexico during and after World War II. They filled a void left when farmworkers went to fight in the war or to work in factories that produced war supplies. McDonnell demanded that growers allow him into the braceros' camps. Using a movable altar, he went from camp to camp and offered Mass. Chavez supported McDonnell's ideas and often joined the priest as he celebrated Mass. Chavez later recalled:

> *I would do anything to get the Father to tell me more about labor history. I began going to the bracero camps with him to help with Mass, to the city jail with him to talk to the prisoners, anything to be with him so that he could tell me more about the farm labor movement.*

Along with teaching him about the history of farmworkers and their struggles, McDonnell also taught Chavez about inspirational leaders, recommending books about people who used their lives to make a difference in the lives of others.

Because of his lack of education, Chavez read slowly, but he did not give up. He read book after book. He was particularly fascinated by the life of Mohandas Gandhi, who used peaceful means to help India gain independence from Great Britain. Later in his life,

Mohandas Gandhi was born in India on October 2, 1869. As a young man, he studied in England and earned a law degree. Gandhi returned to India to work as a lawyer, but he was so shy that he could not speak in court. He took a job in South Africa, where he saw how whites in power abused other races. Gandhi peacefully protested against the discrimination and, as a result, was often arrested. After spending more than two decades in South Africa, Gandhi returned to India and began his fight for India's independence. He used peaceful methods, such as protests, prayer, and fasting, to help his native land gain its independence from Great Britain.

Chavez used some of the same methods Gandhi had used, such as peaceful demonstrations and fasting, to get people to listen to him.

Another future friend Chavez met while living in Sal Si Puedes was Fred Ross. Like McDonnell, Ross would help stimulate Chavez's thirst for social justice. He wanted everyone to be treated fairly regardless of their race or how much money they earned.

Mohandas Gandhi (1869–1948)

As part of the Community Service Organization, Ross was working to register Mexican-American voters so they would have a voice in their government. The CSO had found some success in Los Angeles, where the group had started in 1947, and it wanted to expand, establishing new chapters in other communities. To do this, Ross would need help from new members. As he worked to build membership in 1952, Ross heard about Chavez and believed he might prove to be a good organizer. Ross sought out his help.

As Chavez listened to what Ross had to say, it

became clear that Ross understood the problems of the barrio. He talked about water pollution, poor housing conditions, daily hours of hard work, police brutality, and other problems Mexican-Americans faced every day. Ross believed the ballot box was a solution. If Mexican-Americans registered to vote, they might elect candidates who could improve their lives. Chavez agreed and volunteered to be an unpaid organizer for the CSO. It was the beginning of a 10-year partnership between Chavez and Ross.

By registering voters, Ross and Chavez (far right) took the first step in organizing Mexican-Americans to vote for officials who could help them.

Chavez thrived in his new role. Among his first accomplishments was registering 4,000 Mexican-American voters in the San Jose area. He knocked on doors and met with people in their homes, just as Ross had done. At first, Chavez felt nervous knocking on strangers' doors. Sometimes he got so nervous, he forgot what he wanted to say. But he kept working at it, and he kept improving.

During these house meetings, Chavez listened to people talk about their problems. He explained that by voting they could bring about change. He also organized citizenship classes to help Mexican immigrants become American citizens.

Chavez did his volunteer work after putting in a full day at the lumber yard where he was employed. After work, he hurried home, grabbed something to eat, and headed out to persuade people to register to vote. He kept up the pace for weeks until Ross finally told him he needed to spend some time with his family. Chavez loved his family, but they realized he was doing important work. They would support him throughout his life, even though it meant they would have to make sacrifices, including giving up much of their time with him.

After a few months, Chavez had proved his value to the CSO. Ross hired him as a paid organizer, offering him $35 a week. Chavez established new CSO chapters, first in Oakland and then throughout the

Chavez's children (six of the eight posed with their parents) spent little private time with their father. However, they often joined him in his work.

San Joaquin Valley. The job meant more sacrifices for the Chavez family. They often followed Chavez's work, moving every few months.

In 1958, Chavez was sent to Oxnard to start a CSO chapter. He soon discovered that many Mexican-American farmworkers in the area were angry about losing work to braceros, as well as to workers who had entered the country illegally. These laborers were willing to work 12- to 15-hour days, seven days

Though they provided much needed labor, braceros and illegal laborers were often mistreated.

a week, for very little pay. Chavez felt that growers took advantage of the braceros. Ending the bracero program would be a long fight for him. He said:

The fact that the braceros also were farm workers didn't bother me. The jobs belonged to local workers. The braceros were brought only for exploitation. They were instruments of the growers. Braceros didn't make any money, and they were exploited viciously, forced to work under conditions the local people wouldn't tolerate. If the braceros spoke up, if they complained, they'd be shipped back to Mexico.

The bracero program provided workers for the railroads, which also suffered labor shortages during World War II. During the program, which lasted from 1943 until 1964, about 4.2 million Mexican migrant workers came to the United States, working both in the field and on the railroads. Countless others also entered the country illegally, without documentation.

In Oxnard, Chavez continued to improve his organizing skills. In 1959, he was promoted to executive director of the CSO.

Through the CSO, Chavez made valuable contacts with other Mexican-American community activists. Soon he would use these skills and contacts to make an even bigger difference in the lives of Mexican-Americans. ◆

5 BUILDING A UNION

ᵔᕲ᙭ᕲᵔ

Cesar Chavez wanted to do more than register voters and help Mexicans earn U.S. citizenship. While that work was important, he believed migrant farmworkers could win better conditions for themselves if they united to fight for a common cause. He wanted farmworkers to form a labor union. With the power of a union, Chavez hoped, he could improve living and working conditions for all farmworkers.

There had been several attempts at forming such a union, but all had failed. Many people were unconvinced that Chavez's efforts would be successful. The growers were powerful, and farmworkers were hard to organize because they moved from place to place, following the work the crops provided. Adding to the difficulties, many farmworkers entered the United

During the early 1960s, Chavez devoted himself to building union membership.

States illegally. Since they were not registered with the government, there was no way to track and organize them.

Nonetheless, Chavez expressed his desire to start a union to the CSO policy board in 1962. The board rejected his idea because its members did not view the CSO as a labor organization. Dolores Huerta, who supported the idea of a labor union, later recalled her disappointment:

Dolores Huerta (1930–)

> We were all so sad. Fred [Ross] and I were crying, and I guess the only one that was not was Cesar. As the convention ended, he got up and said, "I have an announce-ment to make. I resign." He dropped the bombshell on the convention. He had so much guts!

Chavez went ahead with his plan to start a union. With the help of activists he had met while in the CSO, including Huerta, Chavez created the National Farm Workers Association (NFWA) that same year.

Chavez and Huerta worked in different parts of California to build the organization. Chavez concentrated on recruiting members in the Delano area, while Huerta based her work farther north in Stockton. They promised to fight for increased wages, clean drinking water, and toilets in the fields. They also wanted to win better temporary housing for migrant farmworkers.

"Farmworkers must live out in the open in caves, canyons, and under trees," Chavez said. "Workers sleep outside in overcrowded farm labor camps, while labor contracts deduct utility costs from their paychecks."

In addition, Chavez wanted to learn more about the concerns of the farmworkers. Chavez, Huerta, and others in the organization handed out about 80,000 questionnaires to potential union members. The answers the farmworkers gave on the questionnaires helped Chavez create goals for the union.

Dolores Huerta grew up in Stockton, California. Her divorced mother, Alicia, worked as a cook to support Dolores and her siblings during the Great Depression. Alicia was a smart businesswoman and eventually was able to buy two hotels and a restaurant. She also was a charitable woman. She often let farmworkers and their families stay in her hotels free of charge. Alicia passed on her values of caring and generosity to her children. Dolores attended college with plans to become a teacher, but the future held something different for her. When she became an activist, Alicia offered to help in any way she could. She often cared for Dolores' children when union business called.

Neither Chavez nor Huerta could have done this work without the support of their families and friends. Chavez's wife, Helen, worked in the fields to earn money for their family and took the lead in raising their children. She also helped with union business, passing out questionnaires. Later she ran a credit union and co-op for the union. Chavez worked many hours, often sleeping only a few hours a night, as he tried to make the union grow.

"I drew a map of all the towns between Arvin and Stockton—eighty-six of them, including farm camps—and decided to hit them all to get a small nucleus of people working in each," Chavez said. "For six months I traveled around, planting an idea."

Like Chavez, Huerta (far right) went out to the fields to speak to farmworkers.

Sometimes Chavez took his youngest son, Anthony, with him as he drove his route. The family could not afford to hire a baby sitter while Helen worked. Often Helen's sister Theresa cared for him, but 3-year-old Birdy, as he was nicknamed, preferred his father's company. Chavez recalled his time with his son:

> *I remember driving up and down the valley with Birdy. ... I would just take a pillow and some blankets for him, and then I'd teach him to tell from the car what kind of field it was. When he learned to identify cotton, I told him about alfalfa and peaches and grapes. ... Sometimes I'd have him all day long without eating but he'd go to sleep and never complain. He was great.*

Though Chavez was often too busy to spend time playing with his children, he sometimes took them along when doing union work. As the union grew, the children stood by their father's side on picket lines and walked beside him in protest marches. His son Paul remembered wishing they could play baseball and go to the park more often, but as an adult he realized how important his father's work was.

Chavez met with workers both in the fields and in their homes to encourage them to form a union. The setting of the meeting often changed the responses Chavez received from his audiences. In the fields, many workers were afraid to talk openly and honestly with him for fear of losing their jobs.

When I talked to people at their homes, it was unbelievable how their attitude changed, how different it was from when I talked to them in the fields. When they overcame their fear, almost all of them would agree a union was a good thing. But almost all of them also thought that it couldn't be done, that the growers were too powerful.

They had good reason to be doubtful. Past efforts at organizing into unions had been squashed—often violently—by growers. But Chavez was determined that his union would achieve different results. First, he wanted to make sure the members felt ownership toward the organization. He believed he could

During a 1933 strike of cotton workers, laborers were kicked out of labor camps and sometimes faced violence. In one conflict, two strikers were killed and nine others injured.

do this by making them open their wallets. Dues for the union were set at $3.50 per month. For many farmworkers, this was a large sum. Chavez believed that if the farmworkers sacrificed for the union, they would have more of a stake in its success.

The NFWA held its first convention in Fresno in September 1962. Two hundred fifty-two members gathered for the event. They elected Chavez president and activists Huerta and Gil Padilla as vice presidents. Chavez and other leaders believed the NFWA needed an official symbol. At the convention they unveiled a white, black, and red flag with an eagle in the center. Some people did not like the colors. Others thought the eagle looked like a bird that was on a cheap wine label. But Chavez's cousin Manuel, who designed the symbol, united the crowd by saying, "When that ... eagle flies, we'll have a union." The members voted to keep the flag.

The membership heartily supported other ideas put forward by Chavez and Huerta at the convention. Among them was asking the governor's office for a $1.50-an-hour minimum wage for farmworkers. Chavez also wanted to start a credit union. The credit union would offer loans to farmworkers, who were routinely turned down by banks.

"We somehow publicized that we had money to lend," Chavez's brother Richard said. "The next day there were about fifty farmworkers outside the door—before we opened the door—who wanted money."

Richard Chavez had agreed to use his house as collateral for his brother to get a $3,700 bank loan to start the credit union. If the loan was not paid back, the bank could seize Richard's home. But Richard believed in his brother's dream. The gamble paid off. Though the credit union lost money on many of its first loans, it was able to survive. By the mid-1980s, the credit union had loaned more than $5.5 million to farmworkers and their families.

Richard Chavez

In 1964, the union also began publishing a newspaper, *El Malcriado*, a name that means "the ill-bred one." The newspaper served as a way for farmworkers to learn more about their rights.

While the union met with some successes, the early days of the organization proved difficult for the group's leaders. Collecting dues, which were supposed to pay their salaries, was hard. Within a few months of starting the union, Chavez and Huerta had signed up 1,000 members, but only 211 continued to

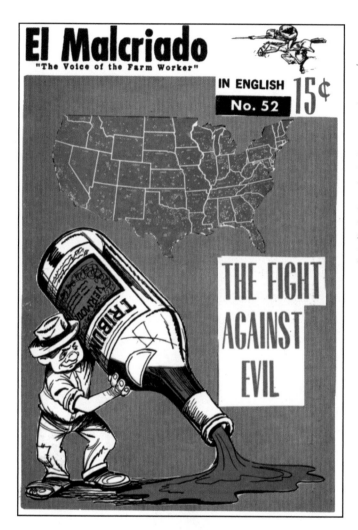

El Malcriado
*took its name
from a well-
known paper
of the Mexican
Revolution
(1910–1920).
On the cover of
a 1966 issue, a
worker pours
out wine. It
spreads across
the page, just
as the boycott
against grape
growers spread
through the
country.*

pay dues after one month. Only 10 were still paying
dues after three months. Often Chavez had to rejoin
his family in the fields in order for them to make ends
meet. But soon Chavez and his young union would
face an even bigger challenge.

FAIR
TO
OC, AFL-CIO
Refuses to
gotiate Wages
and
Vorking Conditions
FARM WORKERS
SHOULD HAVE
THE RIGHT
TO COLLECTIVE
BARGAINING
Agricultural Workers
Organizing Committee,
AFL - CIO

6 ON STRIKE

❦

At first, Cesar Chavez shied away from calling the NFWA a union. To many, the word *union* conjured up visions of strikes—people walking off their jobs and carrying signs stating their demands. Chavez believed it would be years before his organization was strong enough to strike against the powerful growers. However, events took an unexpected turn.

On September 8, 1965, about 2,000 Filipino members of another farmworkers' union, the Agricultural Workers Organizing Committee, went on strike in Delano. They were protesting that they were paid less than braceros for picking grapes. Because the bracero program had ended in 1964, growers believed there would be labor shortages. Government officials agreed to allow a limited number of

The Delano grape strike was the first major challenge that Chavez faced with his young union.

braceros in for the summer. There was a condition—
they were to be paid $1.40 an hour, 15 cents more
than the Filipino workers.

Larry Itliong, the leader of the
AWOC, asked the NFWA to join their
strike. Though he was concerned
about his union being involved in
a strike so early in its existence,
Chavez told Itliong that he would
ask NFWA members to join. He
organized a meeting on September 16 and spoke to the members.
"The strike was begun by the
Filipinos, but it is not exclusively for
them. Tonight we must decide if we
are to join our fellow workers in this
great labor struggle." The members
voted to support the strike, and the
next year, the two unions combined
into one, the United Farm Workers
Organizing Committee. Over time
the name shortened to United
Farm Workers.

> *Larry Itliong was born
> in the Philippines
> on October 25, 1913.
> He was mostly self-
> educated and never
> finished elementary
> school. At 15, he
> immigrated to the
> United States. A year
> later, he took part in
> his first strike—a strike
> by lettuce workers in
> Monroe, Washington.
> Itliong served as the
> UFW's assistant
> director and worked
> with the union until
> 1971. He then devoted
> his time to improving
> conditions for retired
> Filipino farmworkers.
> He died in 1977.*

Chavez stressed that union
members must use only peaceful methods to achieve
their goals. Chavez was inspired by Gandhi's nonviolent tactics. In addition, when he was growing up,
Chavez's mother had taught him that violence was

never the answer. Chavez remembered:

> *Despite a culture where you're not a man*
> *if you don't fight back, she would say, "No,*
> *it's best to turn the other cheek. God gave*
> *you senses like eyes and mind and tongue,*
> *and you can get out of anything."*

Pickets moved from field to field to encourage those not striking to join their cause. The growers responded to the strike as they had in the past. At first, they denied there was a strike. They said the farmworkers were happy with their jobs and that Chavez and his union were nothing more than troublemakers.

"Ranchers in Delano say that the farmworkers are happy living the way they are—just like the

Strikers carried signs that read, "Huelga," or "Strike."

southern plantation owner used to say about the Negroes," Chavez said.

Growers also used powerful friends in the news media, churches, and courts. They wrote letters to newspapers to try to convince the public that the growers were good and the strikers were bad. Police, who also were friendly with the growers, tormented the strikers. They stationed officers at both the UFW office and Chavez's home to keep watch over their activities. They also followed Chavez whenever he got into his car.

Security guards and growers harassed the strikers, too. Some threatened pickets with snarling dogs and sprayed pesticides—chemicals made to kill insects—on them. In some cases, they drove trucks at high speed toward strikers in an effort to scare them. The strikers did not back down, but they did fear that eventually someone would be killed. Law enforcement officials did nothing to help. Chavez stood firm in his belief that union members should not retaliate. The strikers were to remain peaceful.

The UFW was closely tied to the Chicano, or Mexican-American, movement. This campaign concentrated on gaining civil rights for Mexican-Americans. The movement had several goals. Members worked to elect Mexican-Americans to office. Others promoted the culture of Mexican-Americans and spoke out against negative stereotypes in the media. Many Chicano students were moved by the farmworkers' struggle. They joined in protests to show their support.

*United Auto
Workers head
Walter Reuther
(center)
picketed beside
Larry Itliong
(left) and
Chavez to show
his support.*

The tactics used by the other side, Chavez believed, would eventually backfire.

Like the growers, the UFW found outside support. Its support mainly came from the Mexican-American community, college students, and people who lived in cities but sympathized with the farmworkers. To these groups, Chavez was a hero, especially among the young people.

People from unions in other industries also supported the strike. On December 16, Walter Reuther, president of the United Auto Workers, announced that his organization was pledging $5,000 a month to help the strikers.

The strikers' cause also was gaining media attention. Reporters from San Francisco and Los Angeles traveled to Delano to interview farmworkers who said they were being mistreated. All this bad publicity made the growers hate Chavez and the UFW even more.

On March 14, 1966, the U.S. Senate Subcommittee on Migratory Labor began hearings in Delano. During the hearings, Chavez offered several examples of police bias against the farmworkers. Sheriff Roy Galyen, who had served as sheriff since 1954, agreed to meet with the subcommittee.

In a lively exchange with subcommittee member Senator Robert Kennedy, Galyen proved his own bias by admitting that strikers had been arrested even though they had done nothing wrong. Galyen said they were arrested because he was told they might riot. Kennedy expressed surprise that people would be arrested before they did anything unlawful. He suggested that Galyen read the U.S. Constitution to learn about the rights guaranteed to citizens. To Galyen's embarrassment, the audience burst into laughter.

Chavez also pointed out to the senators that U.S. law did not always treat farmworkers equally. Workers in other industries were guaranteed a variety of rights, such as the right to a minimum wage. Child labor also was forbidden in other industries. This was not the case for farmworkers. Chavez said that farmworkers were only asking for what other workers already had.

During his testimony, Chavez told a Senate subcommittee that the strike would continue until the growers agreed to the workers' demands.

Kennedy was deeply affected by the testimony during the hearings. Afterward he met with workers and declared his support for the strike. He and Chavez became good friends. Chavez said:

> Robert Kennedy came to Delano when no one else came. Whenever we needed him, whenever we asked him to come, we knew he would be there. He approached us with love; as people, not as subjects for study ... as equals, not as objects of curiosity.

However, the battle against the grape growers was far from over. ✑

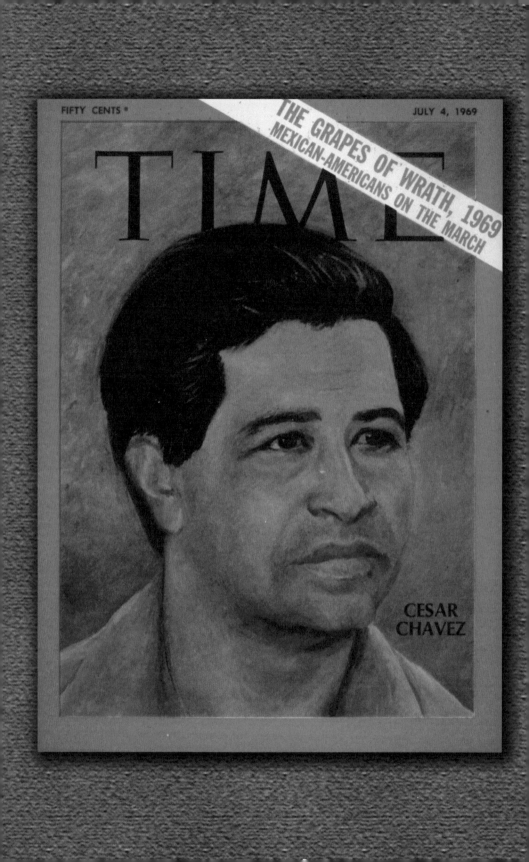

7 A LONG ROAD

❦

As the struggle against the grape growers dragged on, strikers needed something to lift their spirits. They also wanted to attract more media attention. The idea of a farmworkers' march was suggested. After much discussion and thought, union leaders decided their best bet was to march to Sacramento, California's capital. There they could put pressure on Governor Pat Brown to get two of the largest grape producers—Schenley Industries and DiGiorgio Fruit Corporation—to negotiate with the UFW. This would enable them to confront political and economic leaders and have their demands heard.

On March 17, 1966, the 21-day, 250-mile (402-km) march from Delano to Sacramento began with Chavez in the lead. Media attention was high. At

Time *magazine featured Chavez on the cover of its July 4, 1969, issue.*

the front of the march was a banner of the Virgin of Guadalupe, the patron saint and national symbol of Mexico. Walkers carried banners bearing the union's symbol, the black eagle, and slogans such as "Huelga" and *"Viva La Causa"* ("Long Live Our Cause"). TV coverage showed Chavez limping on sore feet that were blistered from the long journey.

Supporters joined in the march at cities all along the route.

"Some people had bloody feet," said Angie Hernandez Herrera, who walked near Chavez during most of the march. "Some would keep on walking,

and you'd see blood coming out of their shoes."

Yet Chavez and the others continued to walk. On March 25, Chavez received word that Governor Brown would be vacationing in Florida during the Easter holiday, when the protesters were scheduled to arrive. Nonetheless, the walkers pressed on, bringing more public attention to their cause with every mile they traveled. Finally they reached Sacramento. The tired but joyous group arrived at the capital on April 10.

"We had about ten thousand there on the steps of the capitol on Easter Sunday," Chavez remembered. "It was an exciting end to our pilgrimage. But we knew that it was only the end of the march. We still had an army of growers arrayed against us."

But the strikers had scored a big victory during the walk. Schenley Industries agreed to sign a union contract. The document said Schenley Industries recognized the union, and it gave workers a 35-cents-per-hour raise. However, dozens of other grape growers still refused to negotiate. Among the

Lying about 85 miles (136 km) northeast of San Francisco where the American and Sacramento rivers meet, metropolitan Sacramento is home to about 1.4 million people. It has served as California's capital city since 1854. Farming has been an important part of the economy in the surrounding Sacramento Valley. Since the late 1800s, the area's rich soil and moderate climate have proven ideal for growing crops such as fruits, vegetables, and cotton. Sacramento became a mining center during the 1849 California Gold Rush.

When he reached the Capitol, Chavez told the crowds to have courage in their fight and humility in victory.

biggest was DiGiorgio Fruit Corporation. Chavez later recalled his concerns:

> When I thought of organizing workers at DiGiorgio, it seemed like an awesome task. DiGiorgio had broken strikes in 1939, in 1947 and again in 1960. ... DiGiorgio had a notorious reputation for being antiunion. So we were facing a giant whose policy was to break legitimate

unions. They had done it before, and they were very comfortable at it. But they met with a very different brand of unionism when they met with us.

Chavez's union would fight back—but not with fists. Some people called Chavez a coward for refusing to harm growers or attack their property. He would not back down from his stance but feared others in his organization might resort to violence out of frustration and anger. To prevent this, Chavez decided to use one of Gandhi's tactics. Chavez would fast. He would simply quit eating until all of his union members promised him that their protests would remain peaceful. It was a tactic he would use the rest of his life. Sometimes he used it to bring attention to his cause. Other times he fasted to clear his mind when he was looking to God for direction.

Chavez began his first fast on February 15, 1968. Later he discussed his decision to fast.

By 1968, Chavez was well-known throughout the country. His fame began to affect his children, who were sometimes teased in school. Other boys often picked fights with Fernando until Cesar sent him to live with his grandparents in San Jose to finish school. There it was not common knowledge that he was Cesar's son. Some classmates assumed the family was wealthy. Linda remembered that when one classmate was told that she was Chavez's daughter, he remarked, "Oh, yeah, Cesar Chavez's daughter. If you were Cesar Chavez's daughter, you wouldn't be here! All his kids go to private schools in Switzerland."

I thought that I had to bring the Movement to a halt, to do something that would force them and me to deal with the whole question of violence and ourselves. We had to stop long enough to take account of what we were doing. So I stopped eating.

Chavez decided to stay at the Delano union office, called Forty Acres, during his fast. He knew many people would come to visit and show their support, and he did not want to burden his family with the crowds. On his way to Forty Acres, Helen tried to talk her husband out of the fast.

She told me I was crazy, and nobody would appreciate what I was doing. I said I didn't want anybody to appreciate it. "What about the family? Don't you think that we count?" [she said.] "Well, that's not going to work," I told her. "I made up my mind, and the best thing you can do is to support me and help me out." I didn't realize it then, because I was too worried about myself, but Helen was stunned. She thought I was going to die because of the fast.

Helen knew she could not change Cesar's mind, so she decided to support her husband despite her opposition.

When Chavez announced his fast to his union

Chavez was severely weakened by his fast. He risked permanent kidney damage by going without food.

members, some burst into tears. They could not believe Chavez would refrain from eating until all union members renewed their pledge of non-violence. Some feared that what Chavez wanted was impossible.

However, Chavez had faith, and he would not be disappointed. He received messages of support from Robert Kennedy and civil rights leader Martin Luther King Jr., who also supported change by peaceful means. In addition, thousands of farmworkers came to Forty Acres. They told Chavez they supported him and begged him to stay alive and healthy. On March 11, convinced his message of nonviolence would be respected by his union

Chavez broke bread with Kennedy at a ceremony that marked the end of his fast.

members, Chavez ended his fast. He announced the end of the fast with his wife, Helen; his mother, Juana; and his friend Robert Kennedy by his side. The 25-day fast took an obvious toll on his body. He lost about 30 pounds (13.5 kilograms).

Also in 1968, Chavez asked consumers across the United States and Canada to aid the strikers by refusing to buy grapes grown in California. In time, the grape boycott worked. In 1970, many California growers finally gave in and signed union contracts.

The grape strike had proved to be one of the longest and most bitter strikes in American labor history. It had dragged on for five years—a long time for anyone, let alone migrant farmworkers who had little if any savings to live on.

"The strikers and the people involved in this struggle sacrificed a lot, sacrificed all of their worldly possessions," Chavez said. "Ninety-five percent of the strikers lost

Robert Kennedy was the brother of President John F. Kennedy. From 1961 to 1964, Robert Kennedy was attorney general of the United States. From 1965 to 1968, he served as a U.S. senator from New York. Kennedy, too, had dreams of being president. On June 5, 1968, he was in Los Angeles campaigning to be the Democratic nominee for president. After his speech at the Ambassador Hotel, he was gunned down by a Palestinian named Sirhan Sirhan. Kennedy died the next day. Chavez and Huerta had supported their friend in his bid for president and were at the hotel to see Kennedy the day he was shot.

Strikers depended on donations for food during the long strike.

their homes and their cars. But I think in losing those worldly possessions, they found themselves."

Though difficult, the strike brought international attention to Chavez and his desire to improve the lives of migrant farmworkers. And the farmworkers themselves could see the results. They could stand up to the growers and win. Membership in the union increased to about 50,000 people by 1970. In the following year, a new union headquarters in Keene, California, called La Paz, was opened. La Paz gave union leaders a place to retreat and make plans for the union. The Delano office stayed open. It was home to the credit union, hiring hall, and a medical clinic for workers. In less than 10 years, the union had gone from organizing strikes to serving a variety of its members' needs. It was tremendous progress, but Chavez knew the work of his union was just beginning.

8 WORKING FOR CHANGE

೧౧౧౩

Since starting the union, Cesar Chavez had received death threats from those who hated what he was doing. As his union's power grew, the threats grew in number. To ensure his safety, a security team often accompanied Chavez as he traveled. For added protection, he bought a German shepherd, which he named Boycott.

But Chavez did not allow the threats to keep him from his goal—improving the lives of farmworkers. He pushed for growers to sign union contracts that would guarantee farmworkers more humane conditions and better wages. He also called for hiring halls, which took hiring decisions out of the hands of employers who might take advantage of farmworkers. Growers needing help in their fields

Though Chavez's fame and scope of work grew, he continued to meet with farmworkers in the fields.

contacted a hiring hall. Then officials at the hiring hall sent out workers to fill these needs, based on seniority—how long the workers had been in the union.

Before hiring halls were established, employers and contractors showed favoritism toward some workers while refusing to hire others, especially those active in the union. Some labor contractors

Without the technology of computer files, keeping records organized at hiring halls could be challenging.

also lined their own pockets by making poor farmworkers pay them in return for being hired. Hiring halls run by the union ended these abuses.

For UFW members, the 1970s were busy years filled with conflict and progress. Chavez continued

to use the strike as an effective tool against the unfair practices of growers. One of the biggest strikes was against lettuce growers. These growers had tried to push out the UFW by bringing in workers from another union, the Teamsters, which did not have the interests of the farm-workers at heart. Without talking to the workers, growers and the Teamsters had signed contracts that made the workers members of the Teamsters Union. Workers who refused to pay the membership dues would be fired.

The lettuce strike began in the summer of 1970 and was marred by acts of violence by both sides. Some UFW members believed violence against growers and Teamsters Union members was justified. The opposition had attacked strikers or hired strike-breakers to do this dirty work. As in the past, Chavez would hear none of it. He believed violence was never justified. Though he took responsibility for the actions of his union members, he was quick to

The Teamsters Union is one of the biggest labor unions in the United States. It is headquartered in Washington, D.C., and also has local organizations in Canada. Among Teamsters Union members are industrial workers; brewery, dairy, food-processing, and soft-drink plant employees; truck drivers; and airline workers. The group has made it through a sometimes troubled history. In the 1950s, its leadership was accused of unethical practices. Thirty years later, it ran into trouble with the U.S. Department of Justice, which believed some Teamsters leaders had ties to organized crime.

harshly criticize them for taking that route.

Chavez was never afraid of taking a stand if he believed he was right. During the lettuce strike, he was jailed for refusing to obey a court order to end the lettuce boycott he had called. Chavez did not falter. He went to jail in December and made good use of his time. He spent many hours reading his mail and books. He was released on Christmas Eve, 1970. Four months later, the California Supreme

Farmworkers kept vigil outside then California Governor Ronald Reagan's home in protest of Chavez's jailing.

Court unanimously ruled that the lower court's order against the lettuce boycott was unconstitutional. The high court also overruled orders that had forbidden most UFW picketing.

In 1971 and 1972, Chavez took his fight to several state legislatures. In California, he helped defeat Proposition 22, a proposed law that would have made boycotts and other union tactics illegal. In Arizona, Chavez and the UFW were defeated in their attempt to force the state's governor to resign after he signed an anti-union bill. However, they did help to register 100,000 new voters there, which led to more minority leaders being elected. Chavez and the UFW also persuaded the governor of Oregon to veto an anti-union bill that had passed the legislature.

The UFW again faced the opposition of the Teamsters in the spring of 1973, when the UFW's table grape labor contracts were about to expire. Without talking to workers in the fields, growers signed contracts with the Teamsters rather than renew contracts with the UFW. The grape workers decided to strike. However, Chavez called off the strike about three months later, after two strikers died violently. One was killed in a dispute with a police officer, and the other was murdered when someone in a pickup truck shot into a group of strikers. An angry Chavez called on federal authorities to guarantee the strikers' right to picket without fear of losing their lives. He also asked citizens to support a grape boycott.

One of his friends, Luis Valdez, remembered that the deaths deeply affected Chavez. "He felt personally responsible … for the life and death of people in the union."

During the mid-1970s, Chavez worked for political change. In 1976, he campaigned in support of Proposition 14, which would have provided funding for the union. The measure failed to pass.

Chavez realized that the UFW needed the law on its side to protect its members. One of his biggest victories came in 1975, when the California Legislature passed the Agricultural Labor Relations Act. This new law gave migrant workers rights in union elections. Not only did it guarantee secret ballots for workers, it also granted them control over the timing of elections and the right to call boycotts. In addition, it created the Agricultural Labor Relations Board, which could supervise union elections and help solve any conflicts between unions and growers. The ALRA still stands as the only law in the United States designed to protect the farmworkers' right to form unions. ❧

9 PROTESTING AGAINST DANGEROUS PESTICIDES

On July 16, 1988, Cesar Chavez, now 61, began another of his fasts. This time he wanted to bring attention to the dangers of pesticides. Crops were often covered with the chemicals.

The UFW clinic often treated farmworkers who showed symptoms of pesticide poisoning, including nausea, headaches, and weakness. Also, an alarming number of children in farm towns near Delano had been diagnosed with cancer. Chavez said:

> *During the past few years, I have been studying the plague of pesticides on our land and our food. The evil is far greater than even I had thought it to be. It threatens to choke out the life of our people and also the life system that supports us all.*

Chavez protested outside grocery stores and asked supporters to refuse to shop at stores that sold boycotted grapes.

Chavez's family was used to his fasting and assumed that he knew how to ensure his good health. However, he became weak within two weeks. His daughter Linda later recalled that the family was scared for him. "The grandkids were very upset ... and some of the union's board members were concerned. It took its toll on us, that fast."

Yet Chavez continued his fast, which he called the Fast for Life, for 36 days. His son Fernando made the official announcement that Chavez would end the fast at a ceremony that included a special Mass. The statement, prepared by Chavez, encouraged others to pick up where he was leaving off—continuing the fast to bring additional attention to the cause. He found many willing participants. The first was the Reverend Jesse Jackson, a civil rights leader who supported Chavez's cause. Several famous actors took turns fasting, too, including Edward James Olmos, Emilio Estevez, Martin Sheen, Danny Glover, and Whoopi Goldberg.

Though the fast brought increased awareness about the dangers of pesticides, it was a topic Chavez had been trying to bring to light for decades. On April 16, 1969, he had testified before the U.S. Senate about the effects suffered by farmworkers who were exposed to these chemicals. Many children of farmworkers were born with defects that Chavez attributed to pesticide exposure. He also pointed out the

Famous actors, including Martin Sheen (second from right), also took part in pickets outside grocery stores.

great numbers of farmworkers who suffered from breathing problems, cancer, and other illnesses.

"There is no acceptable level of exposure to any chemical that causes cancer," Chavez later said. "We cannot tolerate any toxic substance that causes miscarriages, stillbirths, and deformed infants."

On June 12, 1984, he had announced another boycott of grapes. He said he refused to eat the fruit because he knew of the dangerous pesticides used on the plants. In 1987 the UFW produced a video—called "The Wrath of Grapes"—so people everywhere could see the birth defects and other problems believed to

"*The Wrath of Grapes*" was a play on words. Cesar Chavez got the idea from a novel by John Steinbeck called The Grapes of Wrath. *Steinbeck's novel tells the story of the Joads, a poor Oklahoma family that travels to California during the Great Depression with the hope of finding a better life. Chavez could relate to the story because of his own background. For his novel, Steinbeck won the Pulitzer Prize, one of the highest honors in literature.*

be caused by pesticides.

Despite all his efforts, the grape boycott and creating awareness of the pesticide problem failed to gain much support from the public. Through its 20 years, the UFW had called for more than 50 boycotts, which caused confusion. Even staunch supporters of the union often had trouble keeping track of what was being boycotted and why.

While he continued the grape boycott, Chavez suffered other losses as well. In December 1991, his beloved mother, Juana, died. At 99, she had lived a long life, but she always was a source of love and support for her son. Chavez was crushed by her loss.

The following September, Chavez faced another devastating blow. His dear friend and source of guidance Fred Ross died.

Chavez also had to deal with increased opposition, even within his own union. Some criticized him for appointing volunteers to important positions in the union. They believed professional people with more experience could do a better job, even if that

meant having to pay them salaries. Disagreements with how Chavez ran the UFW led some longtime staff members to resign.

Chavez's enemies, sensing possible weakness, stepped up their attacks on him and his union. Chavez soon would find himself back near his birthplace, fighting to keep the UFW alive. ❧

Juana Chavez had marched by her son's side and sat beside him when he ended his fasts. At the end of his 1988 fast, (from left) Helen Chavez, Cesar, Juana, and Jesse Jackson had sat together.

10 A LEADER TO THE VERY END

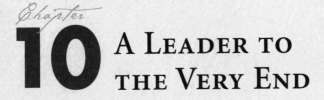

In mid-April 1993, Cesar Chavez traveled to Arizona, the state of his birth. The UFW had been sued there by Bruce Church Incorporated, one of the largest lettuce producers in the world. BCI blamed the UFW for losses it suffered after pickets targeted grocery stores that sold its lettuce. The lawsuit had dragged on for about nine years, and it was a battle the UFW literally could not afford to lose. BCI was asking for $3 million in damages. The UFW only had about $2 million in assets. If BCI won, it would likely mean the end of the UFW.

At first, the UFW did lose. An Arizona Superior Court judge presiding over the case sided with BCI, but the UFW appealed the decision to a higher court. Determined to protect his union, Chavez went to

Chavez continued the grape boycott into the 1990s.

Yuma in April to testify in the appeal. Chavez spent about two days on the witness stand. He also was fasting to gain moral strength. The combination of fasting and the strain of testifying left Chavez so tired that his friends were worried about him.

However, he seemed to bounce back. He appeared happy and healthy. On April 22, after the court recessed for the day, Chavez even went on a tour of Yuma's south side, where poor working people lived.

Later that day, Chavez ended his fast with a meal of rice and cabbage. He later returned to a friend's home in San Luis, Arizona, where he was staying during the trial. Grabbing a book about Native American art, Chavez went to bed early.

In the morning, Chavez's friend David Martinez found him dead. Chavez, 66 years old, had died peacefully sometime in the night.

Cesar's brother Richard and his son Paul were among the first family members to hear the sad news. They cried together, then went to tell the rest of the family, including Helen. Cesar's son-in-law, Arturo Rodriguez, was

Bruce Church Incorporated was based in Salinas, California, but it chose to take the United Farm Workers to court in Arizona because courts there tended to be friendlier to growers. Though BCI initially won its case against the UFW, an appeals court overturned the lower court's decision to award BCI millions of dollars in damages. The appeals court decision likely saved the UFW. In fact, the UFW even made great inroads with BCI. In May 1996, BCI signed a UFW contract.

driving and heard the news on the radio. Shocked, he called his wife, Linda, who told him it was true.

News of Chavez's death spread quickly. Messages of sympathy poured in from around the world, including from Pope John Paul II and President Bill Clinton. Farmworkers gathered, many at their union offices. There they cried and offered prayers for Chavez and his family. Flags in California flew at half-staff to honor the labor leader who had made a difference in so many lives.

Chavez wanted a simple funeral. Following his brother's wish, Richard Chavez built a pine coffin to hold his body. On the coffin were two symbols of the UFW—el cortito and the eagle, which the union had adopted at its first conference as a symbol of

Mourners carried red union flags as they walked alongside the coffin of Cesar Chavez.

When attorney Maurice Jourdane learned about the pain el cortito, "the short one," caused farmworkers, he knew he had to do something. In many other states, growers had switched to longer hoes, but growers in California argued that workers would not have enough control with a longer hoe. They could accidentally damage the crop, the growers said. Jourdane led a seven-year battle to make el cortito illegal. It was a great moment for Chavez when the hoe was banished in 1975, making it an appropriate symbol on his coffin.

freedom and strength.

About 50,000 people followed Chavez's coffin as it was carried through the streets of Delano and past some of the farm fields where he had once worked. Among those serving as pallbearers carrying the coffin were the Reverend Jesse Jackson, Edward James Olmos, and the children of Robert Kennedy. Robert's widow, Ethel, held Helen Chavez's hand as she said her last goodbye to her husband.

The procession finally reached the UFW Delano field office at Forty Acres. Millions watched national and international television broadcasts of the funeral.

At Forty Acres, mourners shared stories of how Chavez had touched their lives. It seemed as if everyone had a tale to tell.

After the funeral Mass, Helen, her children, and Chavez's closest aides were left to bury him in private. His body was laid to rest at La Paz, the UFW's California headquarters.

Many wondered how the union would go on without Chavez. The union's leaders, still reeling from the loss of Chavez, issued a statement that used their fallen leader's own words.

> *Regardless of what the future holds for our union, regardless of what the future holds for farmworkers, our accomplishments cannot be undone. The consciousness and*

Chavez's memory was honored with a U.S. postage stamp in 2003.

*the pride that were raised by our union are
alive and thriving inside millions of young
Hispanics who will never work on a farm.*

Chavez knew that the pride the union instilled in its members would be passed on from generation to generation. He hoped this pride would lead young people to strive for better lives. He wanted them to stand up for themselves and realize they were important, no matter what their jobs might be. He said:

> *All my life, I have been driven by one dream, one goal, one vision: to overthrow a farm-labor system in this nation that treats farm workers as if we are not important human beings. Farm workers are not agricultural implements or beasts of burden to be used and discarded.*

Chavez never owned a house or a car. In fact, he never earned more than $6,000 a year. "He didn't believe you could organize the poor unless you were willing to share in their plight," said his son-in-law Arturo Rodriguez.

Migrant farmworkers still toil in fields across the United States. Figures on how many migrant workers are in the country vary widely, from more than 125,000 to more than a million. Because migrant workers still travel from place to place to find work, educating migrant children remains difficult. Children often fall behind as they move from school to school. Many have to quit school to help their families make enough money to survive. This lack of education makes breaking the continuing cycle of poverty very difficult.

Chavez did share in their plight, and he remains a hero to them today. He continues to be a symbol of hope and courage. He proved that one person, regardless of background, truly can make a difference. On August 8, 1994, President Bill Clinton recognized Chavez's efforts for peaceful social change by honoring him with the Medal of Freedom, one of the highest awards the United States can grant a private citizen. Chavez's widow, Helen, traveled to the White House to accept the award on her husband's behalf.

At the Medal of Freedom award ceremony, President Clinton spoke of Chavez's faith, discipline, humility, and inner strength.

Today the results of Chavez's efforts continue to be felt. Streets, schools, and parks are named in his honor, and the union he built, now led by his son-in-law, Arturo, continues his work. ❧

CHAVEZ'S LIFE

1927

Born March 31 near Yuma, Arizona

1937

Chavez family moves to California to become migrant farmworkers

1942

Father, Librado, injured in car accident, and Chavez drops out of school

1940

1927

Charles Lindbergh makes the first solo nonstop transatlantic flight from New York to Paris

1939

German troops invade Poland; Britain and France declare war on Germany; World War II (1939–1945) begins

1941

Japanese bombers attack Pearl Harbor, Hawaii, on December 7, and the United States enters World War II

WORLD EVENTS

1944
Joins U.S. Navy

1948
Marries Helen Fabela
October 22

1952
Hired to
work for the
Community
Service
Organization

1950

1944
Operation Overlord begins
on D-Day with the landing of
155,000 Allied troops on the
beaches of Normandy, France;
it is the largest amphibious
military operation in history

1949
Birth of the People's
Republic of China

CHAVEZ'S LIFE

1959
Promoted to executive director of the CSO

1962
Resigns from the CSO and starts a union called the National Farm Workers Association

1964
Chavez's union begins publishing *El Malcriado*

1960

1962
Pope John XXIII calls the Second Vatican Council, modernizing Roman Catholicism

1957
The Soviet Union launches *Sputnik I*, the first artificial satellite to orbit Earth; *Sputnik II*, launched later in the year, carries the first space traveler, a dog named Laika

1961
A fortified wall is built in Berlin, dividing East and West Germany

WORLD EVENTS

1965

Leads union in strike against California grape growers

1966

Marches from Delano to Sacramento to bring attention to striking farmworkers

1968

Fasts for 25 days to protest the use of violence during the grape strike

1965

1965

Soviet cosmonaut Alexei Leonov becomes the first person to walk in space

1966

The National Organization for Women (NOW) is established to work for equality between women and men

1968

Civil rights leader Martin Luther King Jr. and presidential candidate Robert F. Kennedy are assassinated two months apart

CHAVEZ'S LIFE

1973
Calls end to grape
strike after two
strikers are murdered

1970
Begins lettuce strike
and boycott

1975
The California
Legislature passes
the Agricultural
Labor Relations Act

1970

1972
The number of color
television sets sold
in the United States
outnumbers black-
and-white sets for the
first time

1975
Bill Gates and Paul
Allen found Microsoft,
which will become
the world's largest
software company

WORLD EVENTS

1988

Fasts 36 days to protest the use of pesticides

1993

Dies April 23 in San Luis, Arizona

1994

Helen Chavez accepts the Medal of Freedom in her husband's name

1990

1986

The U.S. space shuttle *Challenger* explodes, killing all seven astronauts on board

1990

Political prisoner Nelson Mandela, a leader of the anti-apartheid movement in South Africa, is released; Mandela becomes president of South Africa in 1994

1994

Genocide of 500,000 to 1 million of the minority Tutsi group by rival Hutu people in Rwanda

DATE OF BIRTH: March 31, 1927

BIRTHPLACE: near Yuma, Arizona

FATHER: Librado Chavez
(1882–1982)

MOTHER: Juana Estrada Chavez
(1892?–1991)

EDUCATION: attended more than 35
schools and quit after
the eighth grade

SPOUSE: Helen Fabela Chavez
(1928?–)

DATE OF MARRIAGE: October 22, 1948

CHILDREN: Fernando (1949–)
Sylvia (1950–)
Linda (1951–2000)
Eloise (1952–)
Anna (1953–)
Elizabeth (195?–)
Paul (1958?–)
Anthony (1959–)

DATE OF DEATH: April 23, 1993

PLACE OF BURIAL: La Paz, the UFW
headquarters in
Keene, California

Further Reading

Atkin, S. Beth. *Voices from the Fields: Children of Migrant Farmworkers Tell Their Stories*. Boston: Little Brown, 2000.

Cruz, Barbara C. *Cesar Chavez: A Voice for Farmworkers*. Berkeley Heights, N.J.: Enslow Publishers, 2005.

Davis, Barbara J. *The National Grape Boycott: A Victory for Farmworkers*. Minneapolis: Compass Point Books, 2008.

Jiménez, Francisco. *The Circuit: Stories from the Life of a Migrant Child*. Albuquerque: University of New Mexico Press, 1997.

Olmstead, Mary. *Cesar Chavez*. Chicago: Raintree, 2005.

Soto, Gary. *Cesar Chavez: A Hero for Everyone*. New York: Aladdin, 2003.

Look for more Signature Lives
Books about this era:

Amelia Earhart: *Legendary Aviator*

Amy Tan: *Author and Storyteller*

Annie Oakley: *American Sharpshooter*

Elizabeth Dole: *Public Servant and Senator*

George Washington Carver: *Scientist, Inventor, and Teacher*

Madam C.J. Walker: *Entrepreneur and Millionaire*

Thomas Alva Edison: *Great American Inventor*

Thurgood Marshall: *Civil Rights Leader and Supreme Court Justice*

Will Rogers: *Cowboy, Comedian, and Commentator*

Yo-Yo Ma: *Internationally Acclaimed Cellist*

On the Web

For more information on this topic, use FactHound.

1. Go to *www.facthound.com*
2. Type in this book ID: 075653321X
3. Click on the *Fetch It* button.

FactHound will find the best Web sites for you.

Historic Sites

National Chavez Center
29700 Woodford-Tehachapi Road
Keene, CA 93531
661/823-6134
A memorial dedicated to Cesar Chavez and his legacy

Peace Garden
California State University, Fresno
Fresno, CA 93740
559/278-2364
Monuments to Cesar Chavez and other leaders who used nonviolent means to reach their goals

activists
people who work for social or political change

assets
items of value

barrio
a part of a city with mostly Spanish-speaking residents; often a low-income neighborhood

discrimination
unfair treatment based on a person's race, sex, or other factors

exploitation
taking advantage of someone, for example, by not paying a person a fair wage for his or her work

fasting
not eating

legitimate
lawful or rightful

notorious
being well known for something bad

perpendicularly
arranged at a right angle

persistent
continually trying to do something

segregated
separated by keeping one group of people away from another

tolerate
put up with

utilities
services such as water and electricity

Chapter 1

Page 10, line 26: Susan Ferriss and Ricardo Sandoval. *The Fight in the Fields: Cesar Chavez and the Farmworkers Movement.* San Diego: Harcourt Brace & Company, 1998, p. 39.

Page 12, line 10: Ibid., p. 43.

Page 12, line 23: Dan La Botz. *Cesar Chavez and la Causa.* New York: Pearson Longman, 2006, p. 25.

Chapter 2

Page 20, line 11: *The Fight in the Fields: Cesar Chavez and the Farmworkers Movement,* p. 16.

Page 22, line 6: Ibid., p. 18.

Page 22, line 25: *Cesar Chavez and la Causa,* p. 7.

Chapter 3

Page 26, line 9: Richard W. Etulain. *Western Lives: A Biographical History of the American West.* Albuquerque: University of New Mexico Press, 2004, p. 372.

Page 27, line 16: *Cesar Chavez and la Causa,* p. 12.

Page 29, line 9: *The Fight in the Fields: Cesar Chavez and the Farmworkers Movement,* p. 28.

Chapter 4

Page 37, line 3: Richard Jensen and John C. Hammerback. *The Words of Cesar Chavez.* College Station: Texas A&M University Press, 2002, pp. xix–xx.

Page 43, line 1: *Cesar Chavez and la Causa,* p. 31.

Chapter 5

Page 46, line 17: Jacques E. Levy. *Cesar Chavez: Autobiography of La Causa.* New York: W.W. Norton & Company Inc., 1975, p. 147.

Page 47, line 13: Richard Hofrichter. *Toxic Struggles: The Theory and Practice of Environmental Justice.* Philadelphia: New Society Publishers, 1993, p. 167.

Page 48, line 10: John C. Hammerback and Richard J. Jensen. *The Rhetorical Career of Cesar Chavez.* College Station: Texas A&M University Press, 1998, p. 63.

Page 49, line 9: *Cesar Chavez: Autobiography of La Causa,* p. 159.

Page 50, line 1: *Cesar Chavez and la Causa,* p. 46.

Page 51, line 17: *The Fight in the Fields: Cesar Chavez and the Farmworkers Movement,* p. 73.

Page 51, line 26: Ibid., p. 75.

Chapter 6

Page 56, line 13: *Cesar Chavez: Autobiography of La Causa,* p. 184.

Page 57, line 2: *Cesar Chavez and la Causa,* p. 3.

Page 57, line 14: *The Fight in the Fields: Cesar Chavez and the Farmworkers Movement*, p. 116.

Page 61, line 5: *The Rhetorical Career of Cesar Chavez*, p. 74.

Chapter 7

Page 64, line 8: *The Fight in the Fields: Cesar Chavez and the Farmworkers Movement*, p. 119.

Page 65, line 12: *Cesar Chavez and la Causa*, p. 79.

Page 66, line 3: Ibid., pp. 81–82.

Page 67, sidebar: *The Fight in the Fields: Cesar Chavez and the Farmworkers Movement*, p. 139.

Page 68, line 1: *Cesar Chavez and la Causa*, p. 93.

Page 68, line 13: *Cesar Chavez: Autobiography of La Causa*, p. 273.

Page 71, line 24: *The Fight in the Fields: Cesar Chavez and the Farmworkers Movement*, p. 157.

Chapter 8

Page 80, line 5: Ibid., p. 188.

Chapter 9

Page 83, line 10: "The Story of Cesar Chavez." United Farm Workers. 2006. 4 April 2007. www.ufw.org/_page.php?menu=research&inc=history/07.html

Page 84, line 5: *The Fight in the Fields: Cesar Chavez and the Farmworkers Movement*, p. 245.

Page 85, line 3: *Toxic Struggles: The Theory and Practice of Environmental Justice*, p. 164.

Chapter 10

Page 93, line 3: *The Fight in the Fields: Cesar Chavez and the Farmworkers Movement*, p. 256.

Page 94, line 12: *Toxic Struggles: The Theory and Practice of Environmental Justice*, p. 169.

Page 94, line 25: Charles D. Thompson Jr. and Melinda F. Wiggins. *The Human Cost of Food: Farmworkers' Lives, Labor, and Advocacy*. Austin: University of Texas Press, 2002, p. 256.

Cesar E. Chavez Center for Higher Education. 4 April 2007.
http://dsa.csupomona.edu/cesarchavez/

The Cesar E. Chavez Foundation. 4 April 2007. www.chavezfoundation.org

Etulain, Richard W. *Western Lives: A Biographical History of the American West.* Albuquerque: University of New Mexico Press, 2004.

Ferriss, Susan, and Ricardo Sandoval. *The Fight in the Fields: Cesar Chavez and the Farmworkers Movement.* San Diego: Harcourt Brace & Company, 1998.

Hammerback, John C., and Richard J. Jensen. *The Rhetorical Career of César Chávez.* College Station: Texas A&M University Press, 1998.

Hofrichter, Richard. *Toxic Struggles: The Theory and Practice of Environmental Justice.* Philadelphia: New Society Publishers, 1993.

Jensen, Richard J., and John C. Hammerback. *The Words of Cesar Chavez.* College Station: Texas A&M University Press, 2002.

Jourdane, Maurice "Mo." *The Struggle for the Health and Legal Protection of Farm Workers: el Cortito.* Houston: Arte Publico Press, 2004.

La Botz, Dan. *Cesar Chavez and la Causa.* New York: Pearson Longman, 2006.

Levy, Jacques E. *César Chávez: Autobiography of La Causa.* New York: W.W. Norton & Company Inc., 1975.

Mooney, Patrick H., and Theo J. Majka. *Farmers' and Farm Workers' Movements: Social Protest in American Agriculture.* New York: Twayne Publishers, 1995.

"The Fight in the Fields: Cesar Chavez and the Farmworkers' Struggle." Public Broadcast System. 2004. 4 April 2007. www.pbs.org/itvs/fightfields/

Streissguth, Thomas. *Legendary Labor Leaders.* Minneapolis: The Oliver Press, Inc., 1998.

Taylor, Ronald B., *Chavez and the Farm Workers.* Boston: Beacon Press, 1975.

Thompson Jr., Charles D., and Melinda F. Wiggins. *The Human Cost of Food: Farmworkers' Lives, Labor, and Advocacy.* Austin: University of Texas Press, 2002.

United Farm Workers. 4 April 2007. www.ufw.org

Brenda Haugen started in the newspaper business and had a career as an award-winning journalist before finding her niche as an author. Since then, she has written and edited many books, most of them for children. A graduate of the University of North Dakota in Grand Forks, Brenda lives in North Dakota with her family.

Image Credits